26-2

2-00

To William
Much love,
Dina x

Ana Jenkin

Text and illustrations: Ana Jenkin
Book design: Susanna Hickling

First published in the UK in 2019
Printed and bound in Wales by Gomer Press

FSC® helps take care of forests and the people and wildlife
that call them home

A CIP catalogue record for this book is available from the British Library
ISBN: 978-1-5272-3595-3

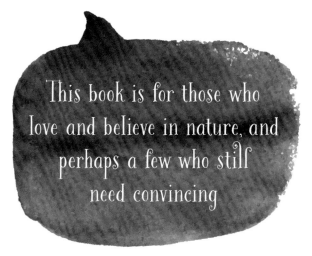

This book is for those who
love and believe in nature, and
perhaps a few who still
need convincing

Contents

5

POEMS

THE END (Or is it?) 60-66

WORTH KNOWING 67-116

Interesting, fun and important facts about
the United Kingdom and Earth

THANK YOU 118

"England is a wonderful land. It is the most marvellous of all foreign countries that I have ever been in"

Rudyard Kipling, author of *The Jungle Book*

We know of a secret lane...

Hidden by bracken, tendrils of fern and dappled shade
Where slugs, snails and insects reign
And in late spring, so many flowers on display!

Ragged robin grows wild here
He of torn but fetching tailcoats to the heart so dear
Forever reaching towards the sun, like the iris
Aloof and ethereal in her fluttery lilac

Then there's the misty blue of sheep's bit
That makes us wonder what on earth is in it
While offering their gold up to the skies
Shining buttercups dazzle our eyes

Mint's sweet scent tickles the nostrils delightfully
Underfoot lies speedwell, the forget-me-not is nearby
At every turn they speak: "Speed well, traveller dear"
"Forget me not when you return here"

Standing tall, foxgloves nod their many heads
As they welcome bees into silky beds, hanging by
The honeysuckle, dog rose, old man's beard
All tangled up since yesteryear

And we, also together, skip happily along
Swinging our arms to silly song
Along this country lane we love the most
Not sure why, but we're off before you can say toast!

8

9

Pan's spell

Like ancient crinolines they spread
The mushroom-sprinkled roots of trees
Their stunted, lichen-spotted
Branches twitching in the stealthy breeze

Soon they will twirl in a ballroom of stars
And the bark of ages will shed
To reveal a sinewy pulp of bodies
No longer dead

Weaving and swaying under a pensive moon
They form a moonbeam circle
We enter its embrace
As Pan sounds his pipes so we disappear

Our shadows follow and then – no trace

Eliza has developed some strange habits
To try and save the planet
Cutting her toenails to stop holes in socks
So she can wear them lots and lots
Same goes for fingernails and gloves
It's years she's had the aubergine pair she loves

Talking of veg, only seasonal will do
No flying her asparagus all the way from Peru
"And Mummy, don't you dare...
(When she starts off like that, she's quite a scare)
Buy bin bags that cause the turtles to die
Recycle!" she screams with tears in her eyes

The local council gets bombarded with calls
Reporting ice-cream van criminals
Not that she wants to spoil anyone's fun
Clearly, it's to preserve her friend Luca's only lung
"Noise pollution after 10pm?" comes the reply
"No! PM10 particles, oh my..."

"You council people give yourselves airs
Yet remain unaware of the true state of affairs"
Poor Eliza rants until blue in the face
Then realising much of the world is a disgrace
She sets up her own Eco Warriors State
Invites the class to her room for a debate

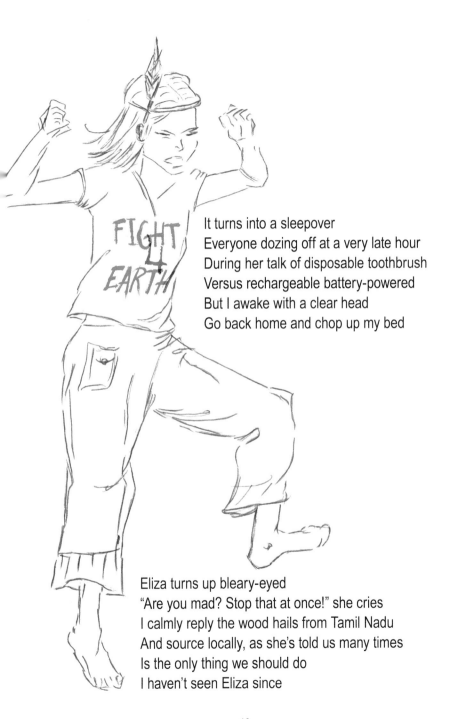

It turns into a sleepover
Everyone dozing off at a very late hour
During her talk of disposable toothbrush
Versus rechargeable battery-powered
But I awake with a clear head
Go back home and chop up my bed

Eliza turns up bleary-eyed
"Are you mad? Stop that at once!" she cries
I calmly reply the wood hails from Tamil Nadu
And source locally, as she's told us many times
Is the only thing we should do
I haven't seen Eliza since

Imagine

If stars twinkled in the sea and starfish floated in the sky
Heaven at our feet would lie

We'd spin as if through air
Milky Way blinding our eyes, stardust spangling our hair

The movement of suns and planets ringing in our ears
We'd dance madly to the Music of the Spheres

Until, unexpectedly, the gravitational pull let us go
To dive up into clouds where beluga whales blow

Then deeper still, to the top of Merpeople Kingdom
Ruled by corals, sea horses, pearls and Neptune's wisdom

Hitching a ride on the smooth backs of manta rays
We'd zoom hither and thither as if surfing the oceans' waves

And when we felt dizzy from these upside-down worlds
We'd happily come to rest In Between until we grew old

Crow Corner

Gertrude has gone
And the shutters of the old house weep with rain
Her little feet will never step over its porch again

Where has she flown? Nobody knows
Silent are the darting red-throated swallows
Mournful the dark family of crows
Forever present as sunlight shifts across empty rooms
Dapples then vanishes all too soon

Down the path, deep in the earthy forest beyond
Fading cyclamen release their heady scent
But where, oh where, they demand
Is the eager nose for which it is meant?

Many years pass and the old house still stands, still
Until one day, the sound of wheels on gravel
Out jumps a boy, all shrieks, wild hair and smiles
Dashes through the weather-worn door
Slides across cracked tiles

And following close behind is Gertrude
Older and wiser perhaps yet taking two steps at a time
Eager to fill the rooms with flowers, hang crystals
To catch the sunny rainbow showers

"Ah, children of mine..." softly whispers the old house
Embracing mother and son, its hearth is happy once again

Raspberries forever

Through the long raspberry patch I run
Down to where the juiciest fruits hang
Ripened by an early summer sun

"Gather some for teatime, there's a poppet"
I hear as I transfer my gems from lips to pocket
"Just leave a few for the wren and bush-cricket"

But I know mine to eat are all the rest
Even when serving the tea and cakes
Grandma gives me only the biggest and best
To squish on scones or chocolate-sponge slices
Mix into whipped cream and vanilla ices

Because Grandma and I agree
Wherever in the world you happen to be
Raspberries go most excellently with tea

So when I am older and she is quite ancient
One thing I plan is to make an adjustment
Grandma will always get the pick of the bunch

We're not leaving

Our home is an old caravan
It's all rather grand
Instead of shopping and dusting
We feed the chickens, make jam
Swim in streams and do handstands

There's no room for our piano
Which sits out in the wild-flower meadow
Attracting gulpy toads, stern stoats, dainty deer
But best of all, a clan of badgers
Whose curious faces draw ever nearer

Our voices are croaky, the keys out of tune
Nonetheless, we like to presume
That applause showers down on us
From our forest friends and a generous moon
So sorry, we're not leaving anytime soon!

a cat

The Persian's hypnotic majesty
A Tabby's playful therapy
The Siamese's disdain at being a pet
A Tom cat's furtive hunting step

Whether you look away and ignore me
Or kiss my ankles, toes and knees
I bow to your strawberry-nosed choices
Do exactly as you please

A limp mouse, flashing lizard, silky vole
Each toyed with before the mortal blow
Delivered by your velvet paw
Then laid down gently by my door

All these I accept for what they are
Offerings or gifts, perhaps
From one of life's true sphinxes

I won't ever try to tame you
The spirit of the wild is deep within you
You may be gone for weeks or days
I shall always admire your impulsive ways

Yet over my ignorance you never gloat
Simply bask in your sleekness and shiny coat
So forgive me when I force you onto my lap
Knowing you prefer the floor and mat

Pathetic creature that I am
Seeking company like every human
I cannot at times resist to pull you from your reverie
O Cat, most esteemed of nature's menagerie

22

The Serpentine Lake

A place of moss, rushes
Most regal swans
Skies cloaked in gold and silver
Billowing across swathes of green
All different shades, leafy songs
Trees rustling in unison

In this realm of air and land
The heron swoops low
Out of the shadows steps Peter Pan
From the hand of Beatrix Potter
Tumble wondrous furry creatures
One by one

But hark now
The night owl sounds its hunting song
Soon a ghostly lady floats by
In velvet slippers and evening gown
As a red moon spreads over the lake
Slumbering fairies awake

To the perfume of rambling rose
Meadowsweet dust, darting firefly glow
Thus Serpentine magic beckons
And I shall make the leap
Please don't wake me
From my delicious sleep

As I looked out to sea
It was just the horizon and me
With no thoughts in my head
I stared straight ahead
Out at the big deep blue

All of a sudden, a shadow was cast
An albatross came to rest on the mast
In its beady eye there was no truth or lie
So we sat there, bird and I

The sun went down, stars came out
I fell asleep without fear or doubt
Dawn brought a strange whistling sound
I rolled over and looked around

There below, in the waves so free
A school of dolphins stared up at me
Hello, hello they seemed to say
The ocean's wonderful, come in and play

Feeling for

I ran to the bow as the ship sped on
To those beautiful creatures who can do no wrong
Lay flat to touch their tails the colour of stone
Until, with a wave, every single one was gone

But in their wake they left a perfect rainbow
Its arc spun from candy floss, lemon yellow
Lavender fields, green apples and turquoise
To take my breath away and hush all noise

Feeling a tickle to my right then left ear
I realised a small butterfly had drawn near
Wafted on the breeze from some distant shore
It was trying to get a footing, could fly no more

Carrying this tiny insect around
I moved ever so lightly, like a cloud
Protected it for as long as I could
Until the wind took it back, I knew it would

As I looked out to sea
It was just the horizon and me
With no thoughts in my head
I stared straight ahead
Out at the big deep blue

the sea

Poetry for Larks

I live with my best friend Sophie
She's as eccentric as me
We're happiest up in the clouds
Where everything's free

In our tiny garret with doves and owls
We're lulled to sleep by heavenly sounds
Woken by freshly baked sun beams
For breakfast we pick fruit from the trees

Sophie works in the city's parks
I write poetry for larks
At dinner time we eat pie in the sky
Then dance and sing for we're not shy

On the first floor are Adam and Eve
They love apples indeed
Besides telescopes, coloured glass
And attending their weekly meditation class

Meanwhile, twinkly old Nina downstairs
Knits us soft socks of rabbit mohair
Whenever her pet angora visits
We shriek with delight at a guest so exquisite

Our communal garden below
Is what motivates us all to go
Outdoors in sun, rain or snow
To plant, tend and watch things grow

Sharing our harvest
Makes us the merriest
Because while two is nice
Six is thrice as nice!

Have you noticed?

How yellow roses smell of lemon zest
Red of wild strawberries at their ripest

While orange roses, in aroma as in hue
Are a perfect blend of the first two

White roses carry a whiff of cinnamon and snow
Pink exude the fragrance of, well, rose

But the artificially coloured kind
Smell of laboratories and we really do mind!

Canine

Twitching when asleep

Heavy tongue lolling in the heat

At the sight of any meal

Chops are all a-dribble

Pulling, tugging

On a tight leash tail still wagging

But let go and what joy

Streaming over the ground

Yet always looking round

To check your love will last

Even as four legs gallop past

Pretending they've seen a rabbit

You know

They will

They'll soon be back

Race over the hills

So let your friend

It's just a doggy habit

Because you should know by now

29

Refugee

In the playground today
I met a boy my age
He said he was a refugee
I asked my mother what that meant
She said, "He's not as lucky as you or me"

Next day he told a story
Of crossing dangerous waters
That left him safe but all alone
Then days of hunger, thirst and walking
Questioning at many foreign borders

It sounded so exciting
I asked him to tell me more
So he did
After that I turned my back to him or hid

Told Mum, "Don't need an extra sarnie
Am not sharing with that refugee boy
He talks too barmy"
Her searching gaze turned bright, "Alright
Just invite him home to dinner tonight"

After he left, Mum took my hand
Explained what he had seen and felt
In his country, that far-off land
Where things aren't like England
And to escape or stay, you had to be equally brave

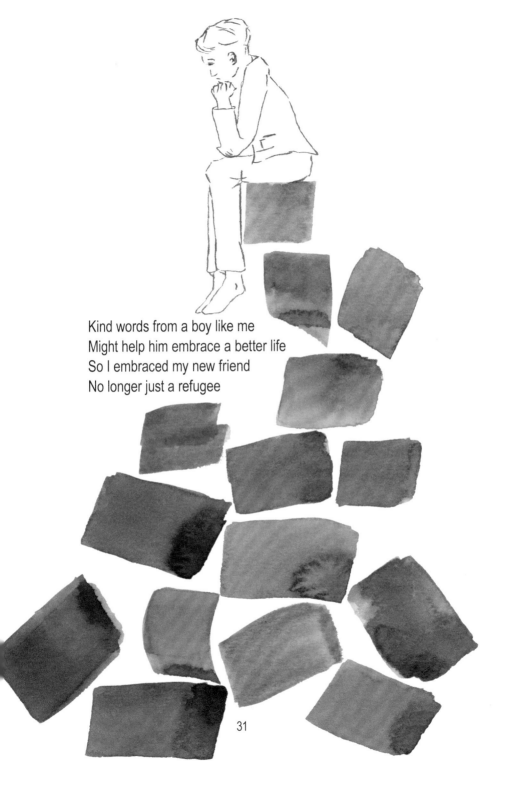

Kind words from a boy like me
Might help him embrace a better life
So I embraced my new friend
No longer just a refugee

Queen of the hill

Leaving everyone behind I race up the hill
Slipping and sliding over mossy rocks
Wind whipping hair into my mouth and eyes
Making them water as bilberries stain my socks

But I barely feel the sharp scratching of gorses
Beyond them, past the big white sentry stones, I know
I shall find my garden of soft purple heather and wild horses
The most beautiful in the world
With thick flowing manes and dappled haunches

As the kestrel and buzzard circle my kingdom in the clouds
I have no need of a King Arthur or golden shrouds
Because here I am Queen of all, when I shout or laugh, it's my echo
That returns to me, again and again
While the others still struggle uphill

An Arctic question

Banished by winter, the sun has sunk
No meteors dazzle the sky
     A dark ink reigns and drips to the sea
     As the whale's grin slices the calm
Thick blubber of walruses rests against ice
Frozen whiskers projecting in white
     Straining eyes in scar-tissued heads
     Near the cream of polar bears hidden in lairs
And the sighs of seals on steamy breath
Melting away night after dark day
     This world of ice floes
     Was it never meant to be saved?

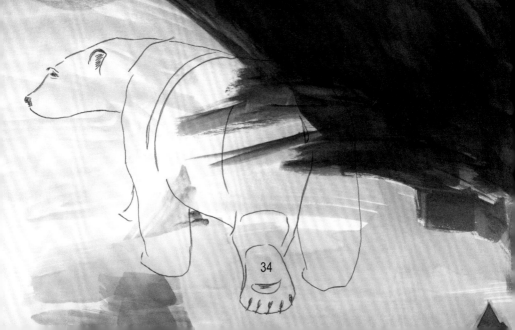

35

How on earth did Grandpa discover the Secret Beach?
Along a dirt track, around a lake, across fields and styles
Then swinging down the cliff face on a ropey old rope
All knobbly knees, runny nose and smiles
Even today on strong legs it seems far out of reach

How did he spot the blackbird's tiny blue eggs?
Five spheres hidden deep inside a hawthorn hedge
So pretty yet cold, the parents having long flown the nest
And the ammonite dug out during a bicycle ride at night?
When all was pitch-black ahead, left and right

How did he find the big bubbly waterfall?
A farmer, we're told, chased him away with a pitchfork
But it wasn't private land so was available to all folk
Perhaps he returned in sheep disguise or shared his tea
Until both were firm friends and having a dip with glee

Best of all, how did he get to the pot of gold?
Which lies, so the tale goes, at the end of the rainbow
He must have set off to find the treasure one day
Returned a year later with rare coins in a bucket of hay
And bought treats for us each time he came to stay

My grandpa the

Just before Grandpa died
He asked that his ashes be flung into the sky
For us to be merry and not to cry
So we stood on the tippity top of his favourite cliff
Threw them into space and did a little jig

The wind blew them back into our eyes and face
Is that why we now see the world like Grandpa did?
As a wondrous place
To be explored and cherished as long as we live

great explorer

Creation: Part I

Billions of years ago
Following energy explosions
Asteroid collisions
In temperatures above the norm
Out of lava I was formed

Having survived this violent birth
I was far from, as you know me
Today's Planet Earth
Shrouded in a primordial broth
For ages I choked and coughed

Until from this water-and-mud stew
Seas grew and grew
With oxygen-producing bacteria
That made breathing easier
So complex organisms developed too

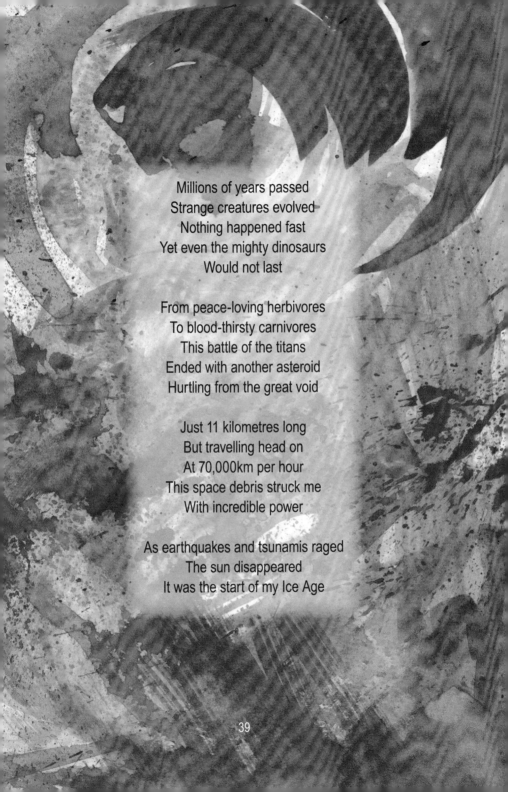

Millions of years passed
Strange creatures evolved
Nothing happened fast
Yet even the mighty dinosaurs
Would not last

From peace-loving herbivores
To blood-thirsty carnivores
This battle of the titans
Ended with another asteroid
Hurtling from the great void

Just 11 kilometres long
But travelling head on
At 70,000km per hour
This space debris struck me
With incredible power

As earthquakes and tsunamis raged
The sun disappeared
It was the start of my Ice Age

Creation: Part II

Cloaked in ice and snow
My vegetation could not grow
All surviving animals died out
Except for a few hardy souls
Which adapted to the harsh climate

Millions of years unfurled
When, one day
I was shaken to the core
Volcanoes were erupting
I braced myself once more

The frosty blanket melted
Giving way to dense forests
New beings inhabited the trees
You may resemble these
I think they call them Hominids

Still my insides rumbled
Tectonic plates were moving
Crunching upwards
Slowly turning into mountains
Vast walls to rain and moisture

Lush landscape turned to desert
Great Apes clambered down
To grow into Homo erectus
Because walking on knuckles
Made them groan and frown

Within 300,000 years
Homo sapiens appeared
Mother, father, son, daughter
Continued their ancestors' search
For shelter, food and water

The rest is history, or almost
As it really starts
With the first human taking notes

So tread softly on my surface
Travel gently through my skies
Think about everything that ties
You to me and me to you
And all the beauty
Which therein lies

My heart a seal

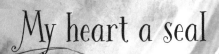

My heart a seal
Its flippers tightly bound
Swims through my veins without a sound
Seeking an escape
Jumps clean out of my soul
Dives deep again into depths unknown
Eyes staring wide
Searching without a torchlight

In the past our grandparents
Were often asked, "What will you be?"
And expected to answer rapidly
"Something in the shipping industry
A soldier... dancer... pilot... clerk
Founder of a Michelin-star patisserie"

But I want to be someone who flies high
Without being told, with others or solo
Generously gives their last piece of cake or gold
Builds for the benefit of the world tomorrow
Feels compassion and dances to dispel sorrow
Is not paid to plant trees, does so to please

The bats and birds who will again be at ease
Someone who is always game for a laugh even
As grey hairs replace fair and eyes no longer see
Just stare
And when hardship strikes knows the path
That leads to gratitude, forgiveness and love

Because, at the end of the day
It's for each and every one
To choose and say
"This is who, not what
I will be tomorrow"

Who will I

WHO?
NOT WHAT?

be tomorrow?

Carpe diem (Seize the day)

O balmy night
Wherein inspiration lies
Whisper precious truths
Let starry visions fly

On the silent wave
Of passing shadows
Carry us the scent
From hidden meadows

Bestow within
A sense of being
Awake us to a world
Of new beginnings

Where each stream or
Babbling brook is never dull
And joy remains
Forever young

Like the taste
Of wild cherries
Plucked from summer's
Soaring branches

Heaven and earth

Up, up and up I go
Lifting into the clouds
Like a swallow
Over woods, towns, meadows
Then down, down and down I go
Leaning forward to nearly kiss the soil
Where beetles roam slow
And little things grow

If I lived for 100 years
I should never tire of my swinging endeavours
Still up, up and up I would go
Until I saw all that was worth to see and know
Then down, down and down
Until I became part of the ground
From whence I would grow and reach up again
Nourished by the sun and rain

Perhaps in the form of an apple tree
Or a tiny bluebell that contains only the best in me

Our beach

Limestone rocks
Barnacles
Crabs
Limpets
Exploring toes
Swirls of smoke
Fresh fleshy mackerel
Blue knuckles
Crunchy sand particles
A cave's shiny anemone drops
Leathery seaweed dragging
Embers dying
As we happily huddle together
Goosebumps on our legs
Sea beyond
Dunes behind
Whirling gulls above our heads
A windy day in the end
But we don't mind!

Tickle

I've tried so hard
And softly too
With brushes, feathers, fingernails
A pencil (blunt then sharp), the cat's tail

Yet all to no avail
Whatever I do
I cannot with my own tickling
That shivery-quivery pleasure woo

Get ranks of little hairs
Spring from goosebumps unawares
Trigger hibernating nerves
And the brain's labyrinth of sensors

So please can I have a hand
Anyone?
To lightly brush my skin
Or perhaps an insect's limbs?

I do believe, if treated gently
Creepy-crawlies were made for tickling
So come, stop your toil
Creatures of the grass and soil

Tiptoe over me, wavy caterpillar
Snaking millipede, ant the forager
Daddy-long-legs, shiny money spider
I love you all!

(Only, I beg you, nothing bigger...)

51

England's green shores

I've travelled far and wide
O'er many a land and sea
But England's green shores
Are by far the best place for me

Beneath billowing sails I was blown
Across the waves of the Atlantic Ocean
Tossed about in the Bay of Biscay
Entered a calm Sargasso one pearly day

Hitched a ride on a one-hump camel
Along the Sahara's golden sands
Grappled with the Gobi's two-hump
All soft fur and flying hands

In the plains of the Serengeti
Lions and zebras charged at me
A kaleidoscope of rainforest Monarchs
Came fluttering to rest on my body

The tropics I plunged into from atop
An enormous elephant's back
Glided down the Brahmaputra
Inside a tiny bamboo shack

On an ice flow I drifted with an Eskimo
Shared his igloo and bathed in snow
Watched the Northern Lights
A many-coloured miracle all aglow

I've travelled far and wide
O'er many a land and sea
But England's green shores
Are by far the best place for me

The Spider Sonata

A juddering of shiny new
Strings in spring
Bedecked with morning dew
And sun glints

In the heavy heat of summer
A dusty frayed tangle
The owner too drowsy to stitch
From tricky upside-down angles

Come autumn, a frantic effort
To tighten the threads
Before chill winds blow and threaten
To topple the sturdiest beds

Finally, Christmas Day sees
This ghostly snowflake shiver
But joyfully, as all the little mince flies
Answer with a quiver

I'm the wind
tearing through the skies
I'm the sun
scorching the land dry

I'm the rain
quenching the earth again
I'm snow
painting everything the same

I'm thunder
growling and bellowing
I'm lightning
flashing then mellowing

I'm twilight
neither day nor night
I'm dawn
shining sweet and bright

I'm every possibility
I'm me

I am

About town

We used to have red squirrels, now they are grey
All the way from Canada, so they say
People call them pests that spread disease
It's not fair, why pick on creatures as small as these?
We'll always like to watch the greys nibbling away
Sleek-coated and bushy-tailed on a winter's day

Pigeons in cities, too, are cared for by only a few
Beggars and old people who share their bread
How else do the poor birds get fed?
But look closer to see how pretty
A pigeon's colours can be, with flashing green and pink
The delicate way it goes about having a drink

And while we love to glimpse a fox slinking by
There seems to be a general outcry
Over the ransacked bins and foxy smell
Yet whose fault is it such animals in our towns dwell?
With more crops and buildings taking over the land
Mr and Mrs Fox have no room to raise their young

As for the latest scare
The common hedgehog is becoming rare
To hear his snuffles and sniffles no more
As he shuffles through the leaves of fall
Never again glimpse his wet button snout?
That'd be a blow, without a doubt

But the worst of this long lesson?
The spots on a ladybird's back are no longer just seven!

THE END
(Or is it?)

All it takes is imagination
to write a poem and do the illustration.
So let's scribble away on the following
pages, then pick up our watercolours, pencil,
acrylics... The result may be great or just OK
— the main thing is to give it a try —
and it doesn't have to rhyme
all the time!

WORTH KNOWING

Interesting, fun and important facts about
the United Kingdom and Earth

 **Wild flowers and other plants are vital to our country and the entire planet.** Around one third of the food people eat comes from flowering plants pollinated by insects. These pollinators, whose own lives also depend on the flowers, include honey bees, bumblebees, pollen wasps, ants, flies, mosquitoes, moths, butterflies and flower beetles.

As well as having a special place in our literature, art, music and folklore, many wild flowers are used as medicines. For example, the red hips of the dog rose have a high concentration of vitamin C, which supports the immune system and gives our bodies a better chance to fight against illness. During World War II, when food was rationed, British schoolchildren helped to boost the population's vitamin C levels by harvesting rose hips. Each child was paid a penny a pound.

"I love this lane, for the roses and honeysuckle that hedge it in early summer, for its privacy... full of broken shadow and leopard-skin light"

Adam Nicolson, writer and environmentalist

Some wild flowers, such as the foxglove, are poisonous but when used in medicines they can prevent life-threatening diseases. Dr William Withering, a British physician and botanist who lived in the 18th century, discovered that the foxglove's toxic content could be developed into a medication for serious heart conditions. More than 200 years later, it is still being used to save lives. Also called dead man's bells, bloody fingers and fairy caps, the foxglove is linked to the folktale that says fairies gave its blooms to foxes to use as gloves. This allowed them to move silently and not get caught stealing the farmers' chickens.

One of the biggest threats to our wild flowers is agriculture. The UK uses almost 70% of the country's land area for agricultural purposes, with England growing the largest quantity of crops and rearing the most livestock for meat and dairy consumption. Farmers can help to improve this situation by reducing intensive farming methods. They can use fewer artificial fertilisers, herbicides, insecticides and pesticides, which kill many plants and insects. They can bring back some of our countryside by planting wild-flower meadows in between their fields. This allows pollinators to flourish and provides birds with more to eat. Preserving lanes and hedgerows is also important as many flowers grow here and small animals use them for shelter.

We, too, can help encourage sustainable farming. We can buy organic food and support our local farmers' markets. Charities like The Wildlife Trusts are on our side, as they put pressure on the UK government to protect our environment more.

 **Britain was once one great, uncultivated wild mass of trees and bushes.** The vegetation stretched almost from coast to coast and was enveloped in a silence broken only by the singing of birds. This impassable wood was feared even by the Roman emperor Julius Caesar. "One horrible forest" is how he described our island when he sought to conquer it in 55 BC. Called the "wildwood" or "greenwood", this giant forest of the past appears in many of our famous legends and books.

"You could almost feel the trees drinking the water up with their roots. This wood was very much alive... It was a rich place, as rich as plum cake"

C S Lewis, author of *The Chronicles of Narnia*

In *The Sword and the Stone*, **Merlin sends the future King Arthur into the greenwood to fend for himself.** There, the boy falls asleep and dreams he has become part of the animals and trees. The ensuing *Quest for the Holy Grail* sees a grown-up Arthur and his knights galloping and roaming through the medieval wildwood. Later, Robin Hood and his band of outlaws will live safely hidden away inside a dense Sherwood Forest. In the more recent but still epic *Lord of the Rings* series, a wildwood landscape sends its mighty trees to the hero's aid. A place of mystery, self-discovery and refuge is how our ancient wood was experienced.

The spirit of the forest is often embodied by Pan. Half goat, half man, this god of the forest has the power to summon all creatures by playing his flute. He first appears in Greek mythology but can also be found in our literature. In *The Wind in the Willows*, Toad's friends Mole and Rat meet him while searching for a missing baby otter in the wildwood. They find the little otter safe and fast asleep in the hooves of a horned Pan. This chapter is called "The Piper at the Gates of Dawn". A beautiful part of the book, it is frequently left out of printed editions, which is a pitty.

For William Shakespeare, England's most famous playwright, the wildwood was important too. In his plays, people enter it to grow, learn and change. A banished duke goes to live in the Forest of Arden, which is a place of solitude and great beauty. And while there is lots of fun and laughter in the greenwood of *A Midsummer Night's Dream*, it is also where the characters experience their magical, and at times unsettling, transformations.

Today we are more likely to use the term "rewilding". Over the centuries, we have chopped down much of Britain's huge forest. Although we can't bring it back, we can plant more trees. We need them not only to feel their towering beauty, but also because we depend on them. Trees filter pollutants from the air and absorb water from the ground into their leaves. This starts the water cycle that provides the rain necessary for the survival of humans and animals.

Plastic has been found in the stomachs of almost all marine species, including fish, birds, whales, dolphins and seals. Many die as a result in and around our seas, as well as throughout the rest of the world. To help prevent this, we should drink tap or filtered water rather than bottled, buy less pre-packaged food and refuse plastic carrier bags when they are offered in shops and markets. If we do accept them, we can reuse them – as bin bags or next time we shop.

"The greatest threat to our planet is the belief that someone else will save it"

Robert Swan, explorer and environmental leader

71

BELOW ARE SOME MORE
SIMPLE YET EFFECTIVE
WAYS TO SAFEGUARD OUR
NATURAL WORLD, AS WELL
AS OUR OWN HEALTH

★**Wrap** gifts in cotton fabric
and tie with string – both are
reusable and prettier than paper
and sticky tape

★**Care for** our own hive – without
bees, humans may not be able
to survive for very long and honey
is good for us

★**Put on** a thicker jumper or
do some exercises to get warm
– turning up the central heating
emits carbon dioxide

★**Put up** heavy curtains in our
rooms instead of blinds – to retain
more heat in winter

★**Paint** walls a pale colour –
we'll need less artificial light

★**Donate** leftover paint and other
unused materials to a community
project – millions of litres of paint
are wasted by households
every year

★**Have** sustainably produced
wood in our homes – furniture

and flooring made from other
materials, such as chipboard,
can release a poisonous
gas called formaldehyde

★**Use** a watering can
or place a thumb over
the end of the garden hose to
create a spray – it reduces water
waste and gives plants a more
natural watering, similar to rain

★**Hang** our clothes to dry once
they are out of the washing
machine – tumble dryers devour
electricity

★**Order** less over the internet –
delivery vans and packaging are
environmental nasties

★**Join** a library – to buy fewer
books, rest our eyes from
computer screens and stop
libraries being closed down

★**Wait** before we flush – if we've
just been to the toilet to wee,
asking another family member
if they need to go after us saves
up to 13 litres of water

★**Buy** low-phosphate washing-
up liquid – phosphates stimulate
the growth of algae in our water
supply, lowering oxygen levels
and killing plants and fish

★**Avoid** diesel-powered ice-cream vans – they spew out black carbon (soot) and particulate matter (PM), pollutants that are very bad for our lungs and the environment

★**Holiday** in the UK instead of abroad – it can be just as much fun and avoiding air travel reduces our carbon (dioxide) footprint

★**Try** not to want too many brand-new clothes – they often require a lot of water, electricity and harsh chemicals to make

★**Pop into** second-hand shops from time to time – it's a great way to help recycle and we never know what we might find

★**Share** household items, such as vacuum cleaners, tools and lawnmowers, with neighbours – anything not used on a daily basis can be kept in a communal shed or other area

★**Reduce** our meat intake – raising cattle and other animals for consumption contributes to deforestation, soil erosion, fresh water scarcity, air and water pollution, the spread of disease, climate change and loss or reduction of plant and animal species. One or two portions of red meat a week is sufficient as part of a healthy diet

★**Give** a friend a lift to school or hop in with them and their parents – that's one less car on the road and fewer emissions (unless our family already has a more environmentally friendly electric car)

★**Read** about nature and the environment – sites such as ecofriendlykids.co.uk and rspb.org.uk look at creating a better world for us and other animals

★**Wash** with chemical-free soaps, shampoos and shower gels – they're healthier for us, too

★**Grow** or buy potted plants and tasty herbs to give to friends – cut flowers aren't half as lovely and many are grown abroad then shipped to the UK

★**Switch off** electrical appliances, computers and TVs – leaving them on standby still uses energy

★**Want** less of everything – it's one of the best ways to help save the planet and make us realise we don't need so much

★**Spread** the word

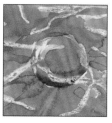 As long as Earth exists, gravity will keep us all rooted to it. So just as it's impossible for shining stars to fall into our oceans or manta rays to take to the skies (as in the poem *Imagine*), so is the idea that we can float away into space due to a loss of gravity. It's just fun to imagine it!

The law of universal gravitation is an important theory developed in the 17th century by the English scientist Isaac Newton. It allows us to understand why our Earth, the Moon, asteroids, planets and stars all rotate around the Sun. Newton realised that the reason is linked directly to why objects fall to Earth when we drop them. In the same way that the Sun's gravity pulls the planets towards the Sun, Earth's gravity pulls down anything that is not held up by some other force. And because heavier objects (that is, more massive ones) produce a stronger gravitational pull than lighter ones, the Sun, as the heavyweight, exerts the strongest gravitational pull.

But with the Sun pulling on our Earth and other planets, it may seem odd that they don't all fall into it and burn up. This is because as well as falling towards the Sun, the planets are moving sideways.

"One of the great joys of science is to understand something for the very first time – to really understand, which is very different from, and far more satisfying, than knowing the facts"

Brian Cox, physicist

To picture this, we can simply tie a ball to the end of a length of string and swing it around. We see that the weight is being pulled towards our hand (just as the planets are pulled in by the Sun's gravity), but the motion sideways keeps the ball careering around. Without that sideways motion, the ball would fall to the centre. And without the pull towards the centre, it would go flying off in a straight line – exactly what happens if we let go of the string.

Gravity also stops Earth's atmosphere escaping into space. And it's this atmosphere that prevents meteoroids (pieces of space rock) and other space debris hurtling to Earth. Even a small meteoroid can travel at tens of thousands of miles per hour. The moment it smashes into our atmosphere, it causes the temperature of the air to rise and the meteoroid itself heats up to as much as 1,650°C. During this process it becomes a blazing meteor, which we call a shooting star.

We can see shooting stars all over the UK on dark, clear nights. Camping in nature, far from city lights, is the best way to spot them. Just by being there, at that precise moment in time, can make us feel very small, but also very special.

The cyclamen and the crow – one looks dark and moody, the other delicate and pretty, yet both have dual meaning. Cyclamen come in many colours and varieties and the most special are the scented wild cyclamen that grow in our woods. In the language of love and friendship, they express devotion, understanding and tenderness. But this flower (poisonous if eaten) is also resilient and able to survive harsh conditions. That is why it also symbolises strength and resignation and may be given to a person close to us who is about to depart.

The crow is one of the UK's most adaptable and cleverest birds. Part of the corvid bird group, which includes jackdaws, magpies, jays and ravens, crows are accused of destroying crops and stealing eggs from other birds. But surveys show their impact is less than we imagined and many other birds survive or supplement their diet this way. Nevertheless, death and destruction are the symbols we have given to the crow and a flock of crows is called a "murder". At the same time, this highly intelligent bird is associated with life's mysteries, magic and the power of creation.

"We've all got both light and dark inside us. What matters is the part we choose to act on. That's who we really are"

J K Rowling, author of the Harry Potter books

We ourselves are full of contradictions. Perhaps this is why our literature and folklore have so many different explanations for everything. We can be over the moon one minute – for example, if school closes unexpectedly for the day – and sad the next – maybe because we think we have been treated unfairly. If our parents are going through a divorce, we may be very unhappy most of the time. In this case, it may help if we can remember that it is normal to feel anger and sadness. Around 40% of marriages end in divorce, so our feelings are shared by hundreds of thousands of other children. Divorce is common partly because, just like us, our parents change over time and things occur in life that no one can predict. They know it is difficult for us, too, so they will be grateful for any support we are able to offer. One day, when we are older, we may be able to understand our parents and their choices better.

It is up to us to be happy. If we accept that sometimes we and those we love need to make difficult decisions, we can move on and embrace all the wonders life has to offer us. Nature is one of them.

 **An adult wren weighs about the same as a £1 coin and is Britain's shortest bird.** Easily recognised by its rich brown plumage and short tail, which it flicks repeatedly, it is also our second smallest bird after the goldcrest. The family name for the wren is *Troglodytidae*, meaning cave dweller in Latin. According to legend, the little wren became the king of birds by hiding on the eagle's back and so managed to fly higher in the sky than the eagle.

The wren has an astonishingly loud song. In proportion to its size, it sings 10 times more loudly than a crowing cockerel. And in winter, up to 10 wrens can happily roost together in a single nest box (the highest recorded number so far is 61). Wrens eat spiders, beetles, caterpillars and flies. They also consume snail shells for calcium and digestive grit. Like many other birds that grace our parks and gardens (the garden-birds.co.uk website lists nearly 100), wrens are partial to wild berries such as raspberries.

Smaller and sweeter than most supermarket varieties, home-grown raspberries are easy to grow. Just three plants provide plenty of fruit for a family of four people, in exchange for 10 minutes of pruning a year and the pleasure of picking. A trick to extend the fruiting season for ourselves and our feathered friends is to snip back half the raspberry canes to ground level in February. This encourages the plant to develop strong new growth from below ground, which matures later in the year. We can then enjoy two lots of fruit: one in August, from canes that matured the previous summer, and another harvest in the autumn from the new growth.

> "There's naught as nice as th' smell o' good clean earth, except th' smell o' fresh growin' things when th' rain falls on 'em"
>
> Frances Hodgson Burnett, author of *The Secret Garden*

If we want to live in a caravan in the countryside, we have to choose a site carefully. This is because, by law, we cannot put a caravan anywhere we want. We first need to get planning permission and a caravan site licence. These rules were made to protect the countryside and to stop people putting up unsightly temporary structures. That makes sense. Why then, we may wonder, does the UK government allow so many ugly and polluting factories, industrial sites, sprawling farms, retail parks and motorways to be built all over our countryside? Some people must obviously make a lot of money from them. But this is no good to us or the animals who are meant to live freely in their natural surroundings.

With nature and all its wonders on our doorstep, there's no need for theme parks. Who doesn't like to play in forests and meadows, spot animals and butterflies and swim in rivers? If we spent more time in natural surroundings, we could even get to know some of our nocturnal creatures, like the solitary stoat. We would recognise the stoat by its white underbelly and black-tipped tail. Also by the way it moves, usually a series of jumps with its back arched. If we startle a stoat, it will dive for cover in the nearest hedge or hole. But, if we stay quite still, its curiosity may soon make it come out for a better look at us.

Badgers also hunt by night, but they are not solitary animals. They live in groups of up to 14 adults in underground chambers called setts, where they line their beds with grass, bracken and leaves. Some setts have been used for more than 100 years by many generations. A badger's incredible strength and shovel-like front paws with five powerful toes, each tipped with curved claws as strong as steel, make it the fastest-digging animal on Earth. The badger's life depends on it, as it digs for food, digs its dens and digs to escape predators.

If pursued by a larger animal, such as a wolf, the badger is able to dig backwards. Fangs facing out for protection, it can disappear beneath

---

"Remember that the animals and plants have no MP they can write to; they can't perform sit-down strikes or, indeed, strikes of any sort. They have nobody to speak for them except us"

Gerald Durrell, naturalist and conservationist

---

the soil in a matter of seconds. But the biggest threat to badgers is traffic, which kills thousands on our roads every year, and culling by humans.

 **It is believed that our domestic cats are the descendants of a wildcat found in North Africa and the Middle East.** Humans started to tame these cats around 9,000 years ago, as people began to settle down, plough the earth and store surplus crops. With grain stores came mice, so people were very pleased to use cats as a natural form of pest control. Cats also killed snakes, such as cobras, and were admired for their grace and poise.

Unfortunately, cats came to be demonised during the Middle Ages. They were seen as the companions of witches and the devil and large numbers were killed in an effort to ward off evil. Ironically, this may have helped to spread the plague, which was carried by rat fleas. It was only in the 17th century that the public image of cats improved. Whether it is because we mistreated them for such a long time or because a cat's wild nature is too ingrained, we can certainly forgive them for occasionally keeping their distance.

> "For he will do as he do do and there's no doing anything about it!"
>
> T S Eliot, author of *Old Possum's Book of Practical Cats*

Cats are still a mystery to humans. Their ability to find their way back home across long distances has not been solved by scientists. It could be a combination of their strong sense of smell and the maps of places they build up in their brains. A purring cat is not always straightforward either. Cats show affection this way, but they also purr when they are scared, upset or injured. Add to this a flicking tail, which can mean a number of things, and it gets doubly confusing. Perhaps this is partly the beauty of cats – we need to decode them to understand them.

Famous cats in English literature include the disappearing Cheshire Cat in *Alice in Wonderland*. He escapes having his head chopped off only because of a discussion: can you behead someone who has no visible body? Even the animal-loving author of *The Taylor of Gloucester* portrays Simpkin as a devious cat. Yet despite being given human characteristics (a literary device known as anthropomorphism), Simpkin is only trying to get to his mouse supper. In the more recent Harry Potter series of books, the "sly" Mrs Norris gets locked up in a suit of armour twice and barely survives after being petrified and hung by the tail.

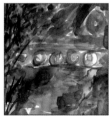 **One starry night, near London's Kensington Gardens and lake, Peter Pan and the Darling children leap out of a window.** The three children are told to head for the "second star to the right and straight on til morning", the direction for Neverland. Written by the playwright James Barrie, the story about the boy who never grew up was adored by the great polar explorer Captain Scott. He named his son Peter and sent a letter addressed to Barrie. It reads: "I never met a man in my life whom I admired and loved more than you but I never could show you how much your friendship meant to me – for you had much to give and I had nothing."

After his first trip to the freezing Antarctic, where he suffered extreme conditions and hardship, Scott returned to Britain a hero. So his letter to Barrie was a very big compliment indeed. The explorer no doubt recognised that while his own voyage had been dangerous and real (indeed, he perished on his second expedition), Barrie's travels through the realms of his imagination were no less impressive. Both explorer and author lived close to Kensington Gardens, which inspired Barrie to write his story and where he chose to place the statue of Peter Pan surrounded by animals.

Beatrix Potter is another famous children's author who lived nearby. She was also a brilliant illustrator. A keen naturalist from an early age, she kept rabbits, newts, and bats as pets, and taught herself how to draw from nature and from books. She spent time in Kensington Gardens and visited the Victoria and Albert Museum and the Natural History Museum, where she drew the exhibits in her sketchbook – anything from beetles to bat skeletons. For a young girl to do this in those days was unusual and she describes her embarrassment as other visitors stared at her. Yet her perseverance paid off and now we and millions of children around the world can enjoy the little gems that are her books.

"Thank goodness I was never sent to school; it would have rubbed off some of the originality"

Beatrix Potter, writer, illustrator, farmer and naturalist

Potter rebelled against convention once again when she moved to the Lake District. She bought a farm and, against her parents' wishes, became a farmer. Back then, it was considered "unladylike". Potter also continued to study and draw from nature, carried on with her writing, and developed her interest in botany and biology. She even managed to annoy her stuffy parents a bit more by marrying a local estate agent, seen by them to be "below her station". Like James Barrie and Captain Scott, Beatrix Potter chose her own path and stuck to it.

 **Pods of dolphins live in the seas around the UK coast and in our rivers.** Scotland's Moray Firth and the River Clyde are home to bottlenose dolphins. These can also be spotted throughout the summer in Cardigan Bay in Wales and between January and April around Land's End Peninsula in Cornwall. White-beaked dolphins congregate on the east coast of Shetland, while Risso's dolphins may be seen off the west mainland of Orkney. On ferry crossings to the Hebrides we can even catch sight of striped dolphins.

Dolphins have amazing abilities. By producing clicking sounds and interpreting the return echoes (echo-location), they can tell the size, shape and speed of underwater objects, which is how they catch their food. Microscopic ripples in their skin help them swim faster, while an entire layer of dolphin skin is replaced every two hours, keeping them smooth and hydrodynamic. During long dives, their bodies use another trick – blood is shunted away from their extremities and sent to the heart and brain. Thanks to this constriction of blood vessels, dolphins have also been known to survive wounds the size of a football, regrowing the chunk of flesh in a couple of weeks. They don't just heal, they regenerate.

Threats to marine dolphins include accidental capture in fishing gear (bycatch), pollution and shipping. By protecting these special mammals we can help them look after our ocean environment. This is because dolphins eat other animals, mainly fish and squid, and are themselves a source of food for sharks and other creatures. Without dolphins, the animals they prey on would increase in number, and their predators wouldn't have as much to eat. This would disrupt the natural balance of the food chain.

"The last ever dolphin message...
So long, and thanks for all the fish"
Douglas Adams, author of *The Hitchhiker's Guide to the Galaxy*

The biggest sea bird in the world, the albatross has a wingspan of up to 3.5 metres. It can glide for hundreds of miles without flapping its wings once. Able to drink sea water, by excreting the salt crystals through glands above its beak, an albatross can spend many months at sea and sleep on water. These magnificent birds live for up to 60 years, mainly in the oceans around Australia and Africa, and pairs mate for life.

The black-browed albatross breeds on steep cliffs in the Falklands. Because this is a UK overseas territory, our government protects the species from habitat loss and longline fishing. Using thousands of baited hooks, this fishing technique can also attract albatrosses and drag them to their death by drowning. It is responsible for bringing the world's 22 albatross species to near-extinction. But by uniting its efforts with other countries, the UK has reversed the situation and this mighty bird is soaring high once more. Closer to our shores, the black-browed albatross has been spotted touching down at Suffolk's Minsmere nature reserve, one of the best places in Britain to see rare birds.

 In the past, many city dwellers could grow fruit, vegetables and flowers on their very own allotment sites. Nowadays, with more of us living in urban environments, individual and even shared allotments are hard to come by. An alternative option is to join forces with the neighbours on our street and transform a disused garden or other area. Local farm clubs may offer activities such as cookery classes and how to grow fruit and vegetables. These can also be good places to meet like-minded people and make friends.

Growing flowering fruit and vegetables gives us decorative *and* edible results. If we only have a small terrace or balcony, we can plant them in pots and even grow strawberries, with their attractive white flowers, in hanging baskets. If we are lucky enough to have a garden, one of the most beautiful and useful flowering trees is the apple tree. As for vegetables, courgette plants produce large yellow flowers, while runner beans, which can grow up against a wall, have small red or white flowers. The globe artichoke produces a huge, stunning purple flower. Growing our own food is interesting, tasty and fun. It could also come in handy if natural disasters cause food to become scarcer in the future.

"To plant a garden is to believe in tomorrow"

Audrey Hepburn, actress, dancer and humanitarian

We can avoid using lots of nasty pesticides and artificial soil fertilisers. Many people think that if they buy food from the supermarket and wash it, they have got rid of all the chemicals farmers use. However, much of what we eat will have been sprayed many times over, from when it is a flower or seed to the point of maturity, so residues can often remain. Artificial soil fertiliser also depletes the soil of nutrients. This is partly why home-grown food is both healthier and tastes better. What's more, we can make our own compost from food and garden waste – it's the most environmentally friendly way of dealing with these materials.

More pollinators can be enticed to our patch. Instead of mowing any surrounding grass once a week, we should aim to do it every two to three weeks. This allows nectar-rich dandelions, clover and other flowers to flourish, attracting a greater number of bees and even a more diverse range of bee species.

Scientists are busy inventing genetically modified flowers. They hope to make them more brightly coloured, smell stronger, bloom all year round and last longer in a vase. It all started with the beautiful garden rose... Scientists discovered it has genes similar to the strawberry and raspberry, as well as the basil plant. It is these genes that make the garden rose smell so sweet, but also provide it with a natural resistance to pests. Experts are now tweaking these genes in their laboratories to create a rose with an even more powerful scent.

Roses have been bred for centuries. Today's experiments, however, involve starvation, cold stress and hormonal treatments. To change the rose plant's genetic make-up, scientists take very young leaves from it and crush them to extract the DNA. The DNA is the carrier of the plant's genetic information or code. Because every plant, animal and human has its own unique code, the scientists use a special machine to read the rose plant's genetic code. They then cut the DNA in precise places. This allows them to remove and "switch off" small portions of a specific gene.

Such experiments, say scientists, will help to "improve rose quality" and "change how these flowers look in the future". But should we not nurture and be happy with what we already have? Flowers of great natural beauty and diversity of fragrance and colour. We can also increase both the fragrance and health of our roses by growing them with other plants, such as garlic, onions, parsley and lupin flowers. As for a rose's vase life, we can extend it simply by adding a little sugar to the water or dropping in a copper coin.

"To paint the lily, to throw perfume on the violet, is wasteful and ridiculous excess"

William Shakespeare, playwright

Dogs were domesticated long before cats. This is because they were of great use to us while we were still mainly hunters. And dogs have retained some of their wild ancestors' traits. Spinning in a circle before settling down is an age-old nesting instinct to make them feel at home, while curling up also helped them keep warm in the past and protected vital organs as they slept. Sniffing scents in the park is another habit from their more exciting hunting days.

Many Britons who own dogs see them as members of the family. Some kiss their pet on the lips and even share their bath and bed with them. While the average owner dotes on their dog, we have started to question if we have the right to keep animals. It may look like dogs are having a grand life, but who knows what they would prefer if they had a choice. They get told what to eat, where to go and where to sleep. In towns and cities dogs are often kept in tiny flats and on a tight leash outdoors. People even inbreed them to get "cuter" dogs. The resulting short-faced pugs and bulldogs look very different from the wolves they have descended from. Just like with people, inbreeding can cause dogs to suffer, as they may develop health problems and illnesses.

"They fed you Pal and Chum, but not that lovely long run. Until, mad with energy and boredom, you escaped – and ran and ran and ran"

Spike Milligan, writer and poet

Some researchers predict that dogs and other pets will be replaced by robots. In the future, they say, we will see animals as having equal rights to humans and it will therefore be illegal to own them. Several countries have already changed the legal status of animals, declaring that they can no longer be considered property. In the UK pets remain the property of humans, but the Animal Welfare Act says owners must provide a basic level of care for them. The Royal Society for the Prevention of Cruelty to Animals (RSPCA) has the power to fine and prosecute people who mistreat any animal.

Lord Byron, England's notorious swashbuckling poet, would most likely not have been happy to swap his Newfoundland dog Boatswain for a robot. In November 1808 the cherished Boatswain died after contracting rabies. Byron, not perhaps realising the danger this posed to him, too, nursed the dog until the disease took its toll. He then had an impressive tomb built, despite being heavily in debt. The words engraved on it read: "Near this spot are deposited the remains of one, who possessed beauty without vanity, strength without insolence, courage without ferocity, and all the virtues of man without his vices."

A refugee is a person who has to leave their country in order to escape war, persecution or natural disaster. When there is a war, whole families often have to flee to survive. A famine, which may be caused by a war or a serious drought, also means people may have to leave their towns and villages.

If a ruler of a country is a dictator, he can imprison anyone he pleases, even if they have done nothing wrong. Often a person's only way to escape imprisonment is to leave the country they were born in, even if that is the last thing they want to do. Their families and relatives, who may be punished in their place, sometimes need to leave too. Many don't have time to pack their possessions. Perhaps they will never see their home or friends again.

While the UK can't take in all the refugees of this world – we don't have the resources or the space – we can help those our country has accepted. We can start by recognising their sadness and discomfort. If one day we ever became refugees, we would also need assistance from other people and other countries. All countries these days have borders, but we were nomads once and shared the world together more easily and freely. In those days, of course, there were far fewer people living on Earth.

If we know someone who has had to flee their country, we can offer to help them with their homework or English conversation. This way they may fit in better and feel more comfortable. If we become their friend, we can also learn from them – about their language, food and culture. We are an island, but we shouldn't shut our eyes to the rest of the world.

"One of the best words in the English language is 'compassion'"

Michael Crawford, actor and philanthropist

Sharing the hills of Pembrokeshire with the wild Welsh ponies is a community of people who have chosen a different kind of life. They don't live off the land, but with it, growing and foraging for their food. Their circular houses are made of straw bales and mud. They choose not to have the luxury of electricity and running water. Instead, the residents walk to a nearby stream to collect their water. Many joined the community to escape the microwaves and radio waves emitted by computers and mobile phones. Communities such as this are searching for a simpler life, like the one our ancestors knew.

Despite the glory of sunshine and wild horses, many children spend less time outdoors than their parents did at their age. Tablets, smartphones, films and computer games are eating into our spare time, says more than one UK survey. But of course we don't need to be told that. We send and receive a gazillion text or WhatsApp messages daily, pore over online gossip columns and snap never-ending selfies. Or, if that's not true, we may be researching all the fascinating information available on the Internet. It's free and plenty of it is educational after all.

Whatever we are doing, many of us are glued to our screens too much. Some researchers believe it should even be called an "illness", all the more serious because so many people are involved. So let's try to break free from this epidemic! Having done our homework and answered the most urgent messages, let's switch off our phones, laptops and iPads. How many hours of freedom will that give us? Enough to step outside, stretch our eyes to the horizon, tilt back our head and look up at the sky. Find an animal shape in a cloud, feel the breeze on our skin.

"Breathe, breathe in the air.
Don't be afraid to care... Look around
and choose your own ground"
Roger Waters, co-founder of rock band Pink Floyd

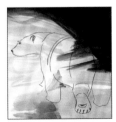

The Arctic is known as the land of the midnight sun. This is because in the summer, the Sun doesn't set and continues to light up the sky during the night. But in winter, temperatures drop to -28°C and the Sun doesn't come up for months at a time. Days are just like nights, cold and dark. The Arctic region consists of an ocean surrounded by areas of land, with the North Pole at its centre. Its polar opposite, the Antarctic, surrounds the South Pole.

Despite the harsh climate, animals can be found in the Arctic. Many live nowhere else in the world. It is home to polar bears, white Arctic foxes and hares, reindeer, the Arctic ground squirrel, musk-oxen, snowy owls, seals (including harp, ringed, hooded, spotted, bearded and ribbon seals), walruses and whales.

The strangest-looking whale is the narwhal, also called the unicorn of the sea. Jutting from the heads of males is a long, swordlike spiral tusk, which they use to interact with other narwhals, as an ice pick and to hunt for fish. Oil and gas development in the Arctic poses a risk to these beautiful creatures, as shipping vessels and noise pollution interfere with their lives. Another threat is the warming of the ocean. A result of mainly human-induced global warming, it is causing the Arctic ice to become thinner and shrink, in some areas disappearing entirely. And the less ice there is to deflect the Sun's rays, the more dark ocean there is to absorb its heat. This creates a vicious circle and speeds up the whole process.

A warmer ocean is a big change for all the Arctic animals. While the bowhead whale may have more food because the phytoplankton it eats grow better in these new conditions, animals such as the polar bear are losing out. The shrinking ice means the bears have fewer places to rest

"We need to save the Arctic not because of the polar bears, and not because it is the most beautiful place in the world, but because our very survival depends upon it"

Lewis Pugh, endurance swimmer and maritime lawyer

or sit while they eat the meal they have caught in the ocean. They are not like fish, which can live in the water all the time, but need sea ice to get around, to hunt and, in some areas, make a den and have cubs.

Ice melting in the Arctic also poses a threat to the UK and other countries. Scientists say it is already contributing to a rise in sea levels, so they are keeping a close watch on conditions. The Arctic is a clear indicator of how rapidly Earth's climate is changing.

 **Our country's right to roam law covers many footpaths, bridleways, farm tracks, alleyways and lanes.** These may be used by walkers, hikers, horse-riders and even those just taking a shortcut into town. The rights of way network has been around for hundreds of years. Part of our history, it applies to the countryside and the city, and makes life happier and healthier for both young and old.

But thousands of these paths may soon be lost to us forever. This is because the law states that any right of way that existed before 1949 but has not been added to official maps will no longer be protected – unless it is recorded by 2026. We can help to prevent farmers locking their field gates and replacing stiles with fences by registering an unmapped right of way. Our local authority, as well as organisations such as the Open Spaces Society, the British Horse Society and the Ramblers can offer advice.

The story of the "pot of gold at the end of the rainbow" is also hundreds of years old. It originates from an Irish legend, which has it that leprechauns (small, mischievous elves) choose this spot to bury their treasure. But since a rainbow can only be seen at a distance, the gold can never be reached.

A meteorological phenomenon, a rainbow is created through a combination of reflection, refraction and dispersion of light in water droplets in the air. White light from the Sun enters these raindrops and is refracted, causing the colours to split up a little bit. The light bounces off the back of the raindrops and out into the air, causing more refraction. The colours then get spread out even more and by the time the light reaches our eyes it has been divided into a multicoloured arc. So to see a rainbow, we need to be standing with the Sun behind us and facing the raindrops.

> "As long as I live, I'll hear waterfalls
> and birds and winds sing... get as near
> the heart of the world as I can"
>
> John Muir, glaciologist and adventurer

Another of nature's exhilarating creations is the waterfall. There is something both earthy and magical about swimming beneath one. Known as Waterfall Country, the Brecon Beacons National Park in South Wales has the greatest concentration of cascades and gorges in Britain. Many offer spectacular (and safe) opportunities for wild swimming, such as Lower Ddwli Falls – a giant arc cascading into a beautiful, open pool. Spray lifts up through the leaves and on a sunny day there are rainbows everywhere. Not many things beat swimming among rainbows and spray, then wandering through the woods, picnicking, and swimming and paddling some more... A tiny bit downstream, Horseshoe Falls has a rope swing for a nice big jump into the water. As for the highest cascade in the park, that's the 27-metre Henrhyd Falls.

 **Most scientists believe that Earth came into being as a result of the Big Bang – a massive explosion of concentrated energy.** This explosion, which is thought to have happened 13.7 billion years ago, first created our Universe. Then, as asteroids collided and produced gravitational mass, Earth was slowly formed. Initially a boiling ball of fire and lava, our planet cooled down and seas appeared. Single-celled creatures evolved first, followed by more complex, multi-cellular forms of life, including plants and animals.

By the Jurassic period, the dinosaurs were the most powerful creatures on Earth. Recent research has discovered that the biggest ever carnivorous dinosaur was the Spinosaurus, followed by the Giganotosaurus and the Tyrannosaurus. But while the Spinosaurus, which was able to swim, could reach 18 metres in length and weigh nine tonnes, the fact that its teeth were not jagged leads scientists to believe it mainly survived on fish and carcasses. Both the Giganotosaurus and the Tyrannosaurus had serrated, eight-inch-long teeth, which could easily tear into the flesh of other animals. They also had a keen sense of smell and good vision.

Although the Giganotosaurus was more agile, the Tyrannosaurus's jaws were far more powerful and it had a larger brain. In fact, the brain of the Giganotosaurus – in size and shape resembling a banana – was small compared to its skull, which makes scientists think it would have had more success hunting large prey in packs. So overall, even if not the largest, the Tyrannosaurus has managed to keep its place as the most formidable predator in dinosaur history.

After the collision between an enormous asteroid and Earth, none of these giants, encumbered by their bodies and food requirements, survived. Instead, it was the smaller, flying dinosaurs that pulled through. Called maniraptorans, this group of feathered dinosaurs had originally been much bigger. Over time, as most of the land-bound dinosaurs grew ever larger, the maniraptorans diminished in size. When conditions and habitats drastically changed, they were able to adapt more easily. Gradually, they evolved into the birds we know and love today.

"We can't understand life, unless we understand what it's all there for, how it arose – and that means evolution"

Richard Dawkins, evolutionary biologist

But science is forever asking questions. What if the asteroid had missed our planet and one of the big ice ages had never happened? Would dinosaurs be here today? What new dinosaurs might have appeared? Would they have developed human-like intelligence? Would humans ever have evolved? And if so, would they have found a way to survive alongside the dinosaurs? Or, looking to the future, and the potential scarcity of food and fresh water, will humans start to diminish in size like the maniraptorans did?

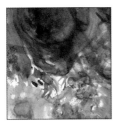 **At least five major ice ages have occurred throughout Earth's history and we are living in one right now.** Unlike the big freeze following the huge collision between Earth and the asteroid, our current Ice Age began around three million years ago and is happening gradually. Yet its effects, say scientists, are not being felt because of humans. Over the past 50 years or so, the sun has indeed been slightly less bright and has therefore been emitting less energy. In a previous ice age, this would have resulted in a small drop in Earth's overall surface temperature. Today, however, the natural process is being reversed because of manmade global warming.

The biggest culprit is emissions from cars, lorries, planes, agriculture, factories, our homes and businesses. These emissions, mainly carbon dioxide and methane, as well as some other gases, act to retain heat in the atmosphere. They are generally called greenhouse gases and scientists have noted that they have contributed to a small but significant rise in Earth's surface temperature. If we carry on living the way we do, they warn, we may contribute to a further increase in temperature and the consequences could be dramatic. So while it would take millions of years for another full-blown ice age to occur, global warming is a much more immediate cause for concern.

Our closest extinct human relatives, the Neanderthals, managed to survive in extremely hostile and changing environments. In fact, they spent 250,000 years or more living in the harshest climates. Similarly to us, they were extremely resourceful. When Earth was encased in snow and ice, they mastered the use of fire and invented clothing to keep warm. As for our ancestors, these were the early modern humans who lived after the Neanderthals eventually died out. Having reached Britain around 30,000 years ago, they survived the last ice age by heading to warmer continents. They gradually came back as the climate returned to more normal conditions.

Our ancestors lived in a world where a nomadic lifestyle was the norm, moving with the seasons in search of food and water. So travelling much further afield, whenever climate conditions became more extreme, must also have been a natural choice for them. The question for us now is: can we turn back the clock on manmade climate and other changes, and if not, how can we and future generations adapt?

"After 4.5 billion years of existence, Earth's fate may be determined this century by one species alone – ours"

Martin Rees, cosmologist and space scientist

If each reader of this book chose to support just one of the following organisations or initiatives, together we could help save something precious.

★**The Badger Trust** Teaches us about this impressive animal and opposes widespread culling

★**The Barn Owl Trust** Its mission is to conserve one of the UK's most beautiful birds

★**British Beekeepers Association** Promotes beekeeping, which is crucial to our environment

★**Buglife** Seeks to save Britain's

invertebrates, from beetles and worms to spiders and jellyfish

★The Bumblebee Conservation Trust Aims to improve the plight of the bumblebee

★Butterfly Conservation Set up in 1968 due to the decline of butterflies

★Campaign to Protect Rural England Fights for a countryside we can all enjoy

★Forestry Commission Scotland Manages forests and woodland in a sustainable way

★Froglife Gives frogs, toads, newts, snakes and lizards a better chance of survival

★Game and Wildlife Conservation Trust Advises farmers in the UK how to improve wildlife habitats

★Hedgehog Street Raises awareness about our wobbly hedgehog situation

★Marine Conservation Society Looks after the UK's seas, shores and wildlife

★The National Marine Aquarium Protects marine and freshwater organisms

★The National Trust Founded in 1895, it opposes uncontrolled development and industrialisation

★The Penllergare Trust Conserves wildlife in this beautiful region of Wales

★Plantlife Brings people together to help bring back our wild flowers

★Royal Society for the Protection of Birds Works to save threatened birds and wildlife

★Royal Zoological Society of Scotland Promotes the conservation of endangered animals in the UK and worldwide

★Scottish Environment Link Encourages a more environmentally friendly society

★Scottish Wildlife Trust Supports nature conservation throughout Scotland

★Sea Shepherd UK Stops the destruction of marine wildlife across the world's oceans

★SongBird Survival Funds

research into the alarming decline in Britain's songbirds

★Sustrans A charity that makes it easier for people to walk and cycle

★The Vincent Wildlife Trust Helps safeguard the future of mammals in the UK and Ireland

★The Wildlife Trust of South and West Wales Manages beautiful areas, from islands to ancient woodland

★The Wildlife Trusts Care for 2,300 reserves, including woods, rivers and city parks

---

"What you do makes a difference and you need to decide what kind of difference you want to make"

Jane Goodall, primatologist

Nearly half of all the world's grey seals live in the coastal waters of the UK. Female grey seals haul themselves ashore to give birth in autumn and winter. Having feasted on fish all summer, it is the time they are at their fittest and healthiest to feed their pups milk. As soon as a pup is born, the mother spins round to sniff it and get to know its smell. So we should not touch pups, or any other wild baby animals for that matter. We may leave our scent and if the mother does not recognise the baby as her own, it risks being abandoned.

The white fur it is born with makes a grey seal pup even more vulnerable, as it provides no camouflage on a sandy or pebbly beach. A newborn seal's white fur is a remnant of the last ice age, when it would have blended in with the snow and ice. After a month, once their mothers have headed back out to sea, the pups are left alone on the shore. It takes around two weeks for their white coat to be replaced with a grey one, after which they are ready to take the plunge and learn to fish for themselves.

The pupping season for grey seals starts as early as August in Cornwall. In Wales it is September to October, and pups are born from November to December in Scotland and down the East coast of England. With their curious nature and cuddly appearance, the pups are a delight to watch as they bask in coves and on beaches. But they have sharp teeth, another reason to keep our distance and show respect for these wild animals. The best way to see them is by joining a seal-viewing expedition, which can also introduce us to our other native breeding seal. Called the common seal, its pups are born without a white coat and can swim almost immediately.

SEAL is a fun and interesting way to learn in school. The word stands for Social and Emotional Aspects of Learning, which may sound a bit serious but in fact allows us to be more creative. Through dance, acting, poetry and singing, we get to express ourselves and boost our confidence. We can then learn better and more easily. For example, we may be a character or an animal in a play, song or poem, which means that, for a short while, we get closer to how that person or animal

"I'm not an animal lover if that means you think things are nice if you can pat them, I am intoxicated by animals"

David Attenborough, natural historian

behaves and thinks. Or maybe we just want to explain what it feels like to be us. Learning the SEAL way can open all kinds of doors as it helps us to understand ourselves and others.

A recent survey discovered that nearly 40% of British working adults believe their job is meaningless. "It's as if someone were out there making up pointless jobs for the sake of keeping us all working," reads one statement. It's worth thinking about, because we want to avoid being among those 40% one day. Finding out early on what makes ourselves and others feel good gives us a head start.

We could volunteer at our local charity sale or pet shelter. Go blackberry picking, then make blackberry and apple jam to share among our friends. Take an elderly neighbour's dog to the vet for a claw trim. Visit the Woodland Trust website to see how we can go about planting a tree or, if we want to think big, a small forest. Join a hiking group to climb a mountain. Become a Scout to learn how to survive in the wild. Being close to people and nature gives meaning to our lives. We are then better equipped to one day have a meaningful job.

"One of the reasons I became a Scout was to spend more time with friends in the outdoors. It's among the greatest experiences in life"
Bear Grylls, adventurer and TV presenter

HERE ARE JUST A FEW WORTHWHILE JOBS TO KEEP AT THE BACK OF OUR MINDS

★wildlife biologist
★environmental lawyer
★urban farmer
★clean water modeller
★hydrogeologist
★marine consents manager
★forestry engineer
★landscape architect
★environmental scientist
★animal shelter manager
★biodiversity project officer
★investigative journalist
★veterinary nurse
★marine botanist
★Green Party politician
★entomologist
★community education officer
★anthrozoologist
★work health and safety consultant
★meteorologist
★alternative therapist
★town planner
★Smart Buildings engineer

★geologist
★air quality consultant
★conservation scientist
★ethnobotanist
★arboricultural surveyor
★socio-economics specialist
★landfill site manager
★animal lawyer
★sustainability data analyst
★ecologist
★waste materials specialist
★wind farm engineer
★energy economist
★community wildlife assistant
★conservation fundraiser
★woodland officer
★organic farming and products regulator
★community care worker
★climate finance adviser
★ornithologist
★renewable energy surveyor
★gardener
★environmental writer
★coastal engineer
★well-being consultant

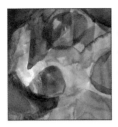

Despite many studies, no one knows yet exactly why we dream. Researchers believe it helps us to solve problems and understand our feelings and thoughts. In other words, dreams can make us feel better psychologically and they may even make us more creative.

According to neuroscientists (scientists who study the brain), sleep associated with dreams is also physiological (linked to the body). A great deal of brain activity occurs while we sleep, especially during the second half of our night's sleep. Scientists say this is due to the brain warming its "circuits" in order to prepare our body for the sights, sounds and emotions we will experience when we awake. A rude awakening by a screeching alarm clock is, therefore, probably best avoided.

"Sometimes, though not often, he had dreams, and they were more painful than the dreams of other boys. They had to do, I think, with the riddle of his existence"

J M Barrie, author of *Peter Pan*

Some people, adults and children alike, suffer from insomnia. This is when we regularly get less than five or six hours of sleep a night. We should try to deal with our insomnia, as it interferes with our rest and our dreams and changes how we feel on waking. It can help if we do some exercise earlier in the day, such as swimming or running, don't go to bed too late, switch off all our gadgets and screens at least one hour before and ensure our feet are warm. And if we want to have more vivid dreams, according to some experts, nibbling a piece of Cheddar cheese does the trick.

If we've had a good night's sleep and it happens to be July, we can use all our bags of energy to go cherry picking. Thanks to Henry VIII, who ordered cherry orchards to be planted in Kent, this part of England is full of cherries – from white Amber to black Morello. What's more, the people of Kent have also managed to keep many traditional organic orchards. These produce the tastiest and healthiest cherries and are best eaten straight from the tree. Or we can do as the Romans did and serve them floating in a bowl of iced water. Because even before Henry VIII, cherries made their way to England via the Romans. It is said that many Roman roads had cherry trees along their length, sprouted from the stones spat by marching legions.

If we prefer our cherries slightly sour, we can head for the beech woods and hedgerows where the wild cherry trees grow. Found across the UK, this native species also provides food for many creatures – from bees and birds to dormice and badgers.

The Big Rush is 88 metres high and the tallest rope swing in the world, according to *The Guinness Book of Records*. Located at the Moses Mabhida Stadium in Durban, South Africa, it can reach speeds of up to 90 miles per hour. But there's no need to go in for such stomach-churning experiences. Swinging on a swing closer to home, and to the ground, lifts the spirits and creates the feel-good hormones endorphins. It's even better if done on a sunny day, in green surroundings and in good company. But as they get older, people often forget the simple joys of youth, so the trick is never to resist a swing when we see one.

"We do not stop playing because we grow old;
we grow old because we stop playing"

George Bernard Shaw, playwright and political activist

The barn swallow is the songbird and acrobat who commands immaculate flight. It zooms about at up to 15 metres per second and dives down to within a couple of centimetres of the water's surface. On a summer's afternoon, one may gaze for hours at these aerial insectivores, their feathers flashing as they snap up insects mid-air and miraculously avoid collisions. Swallows grace our shores from Africa, where they return to escape the harsh winters. They are often confused with swifts, which hold the record for the fastest of all birds in level flight.

At around the same time, bluebell flowers cloak our forest floors with their multitude of tiny bowing heads. In Scotland, the name bluebell is often used to refer to the larger and less vibrantly coloured harebell flower, believed in the past to hide witches once they had turned themselves into hares. And in Victorian times, when people communicated their feelings with flowers, the bluebell was given to someone to express gratitude. We've lost these traditions, but it's worth remembering them. Perhaps all the more so since our native bluebell is being threatened by the loss of ancient woodland and the spread of an invasive Spanish species. Unlike our native, which has a string of bells only on one side of the stem, the Spanish bluebell has bells on either side. Both species, however, are poisonous if eaten.

The sand grains on a beach are formed over many thousands and millions of years. It happens when surrounding rock and ocean-floor sediments are broken down by waves. Coastal winds and storms then push these sediments up beyond the reach of the waves and a beach is born. Beaches with fine sand take longer to form and so are older than beaches with pebbles or coarse sand.

We don't have to get on a plane to discover stunning beaches. The UK coastline has more than 6,000 kilometres of shoreline, the point at which sea meets land and along which beaches can be found. Sandwood Bay in north-west Scotland has pinky-orange sand – from the erosion of red sandstone cliffs – and emerald shallows. In England's south-west, the surreally beautiful Porthcurno beach in Cornwall is made almost entirely from ground seashells. Its pale honey colour is lapped by turquoise

"There is a pleasure in the pathless woods, there is a rapture on the lonely shore, there is society, where none intrudes, by the deep Sea, and music in its roar; I love not Man the less, but Nature more"

George Byron, poet

waters and backed by granite cliffs. For extra-soft, centuries-old sand, the pristine Barafundel Bay in Wales' Pembrokeshire beckons.

As the tide comes in and retreats from a beach, it leaves behind seaweed, driftwood and dead plants and animals. All of this helps to create and support our unique shoreline habitats. The seaweed breaks down, producing organic matter and providing nutrients for sand dunes and other plants. It is also a rich food source for many creatures, including sand hoppers, beetles and crabs. Bits of driftwood offer shelter and certain beetles feed only on sea-soaked wood. The kelp fly lays its eggs on beaches and the emerging maggots become food for other beetles and birds. The birds we can spot feeding along the shoreline include dunlin, oystercatcher, ringed plover, sanderling and turnstone.

Rising sea levels increase the risk of flooding in human-populated areas. Sea walls and other sea defences have to be built, which ruins our beaches and shorelines. Another threat is pollution from agricultural chemicals and rubbish brought by the tides. If mechanical beach cleaning is used, the heavy machinery removes the top 10 to 15 centimetres of sand containing creatures and organic matter. Hand cleaning, however, preserves the beach ecosystem. Some Wildlife Trusts organise beach cleans, so we can volunteer and get involved.

There is a scientific reason why we get goosebumps when we are being gently tickled. Researchers believe that goosebumps, which cause our hairs to stand on end, originated in the distant past. They may have helped us insulate ourselves against the cold. But they may also have made us appear bigger to scare off predators and prepared us to take flight when we felt threatened. Today, as a reflex retained from our ancestors, we still get goosebumps when we're frightened or cold. But it happens when we are being pleasurably tickled, too. According to researchers, this is down to the C nerve fibres located in our brain. As long as we are stroked gently, at just four centimetres per second, the nerve fibres record pleasure. But because they are still associated with our ancestors' "fight or flight" instincts, they also cause our hairs to stand on end. The result? Goosebumps.

"I dug things up. I was curious. There is so much we do not know"

Mary Leakey, fossil hunter and anthropologist

Other scientists have focused their attention on the millipede.
Bus driver and amateur fossil collector Mike Newman came across the remains of one dating back more than 400 million years. Discovered in siltstone in Scotland, the millipede was named after him: *Pneumodesmus newmani*. It is the earliest animal found to be adapted to air-breathing and life on land. This is thanks to its spiracles, holes that absorb oxygen directly from the air into the body. Today's millipedes, which are related to insects, breathe in the same way. Important for the health of forests and other habitats, millipedes feed on last year's leaves, recycling the nutrients and enriching the soil.

Insects can also help us solve problems. Take the caterpillar's flexible body, which moves in undulating waves. Biologists have discovered that this astonishing freedom of movement is due to the caterpillar's insides shifting independently and in advance of its body and legs. These findings are influencing the design of soft-bodied robots, which can perform differently to robots with a rigid skeleton. For example, they may be used in sea search-and-rescue missions, as their flexible bodies allow them to pass through tight spaces. They would also be able to handle live creatures more gently.

The last Roman soldiers departed from Britain in AD 410. The native Celtic Britons were then joined by new people arriving in ships across the North Sea. These were the Anglo-Saxon settlers, originally from tribes in north Germany, Denmark and the Netherlands. Historians view their arrival as the origin of England and of the English people.

Viking tribes carried out the greatest number of invasions on English soil. These took place between the 8th and 11th centuries under the leadership of such scary individuals as Björn Ironside and William Bloodaxe. The last conquest was by William the Conqueror, head of the Viking Normans in France. He became King of England and permanently changed the English language and culture. Louis VIII of France also tried to take power over England in the early 13th century and later Spain made an attempt, but its armada was defeated by a storm before it reached our shores. Neither was Hitler to get far during World War II.

Today's United Kingdom contains four nations. These include England, Scotland and Wales, which make up Great Britain, and Northern Ireland, which was once part of Ireland. All four countries have their own national flag, although Northern Ireland is often referred to as a province, rather than a country in its own right. In the past, a great deal of blood was spilt due to the English, Scottish and Welsh fighting among themselves. Many territorial wars were fought between Scotland and England during the 12th, 13th and 14th centuries. In 1328 Scotland gained its independence. Although the following centuries still witnessed repeat battles with England, the two countries united in 1707 and the United Kingdom of Great Britain was created.

Wales was also ruled by England in the past. By the 16th century, it had merged with England. Cymru is the Welsh word for Wales and means "friends" or "fellow countrymen". The word Wales, by which most people know the country, stems from a word used by the invading Anglo-Saxons to mean "foreigners" or "outsiders", despite the Welsh being native to the land. And despite England's dominance and Wales having led revolts against its rule in the past, the Welsh have retained their language and culture.

"It's always good to remember where you come from and celebrate it. To remember where you come from is part of where you're going"

Anthony Burgess, writer and composer

Ireland used to be part of the United Kingdom. The English were involved in the rule of Ireland since the 12th century and in 1801 Ireland formally joined the UK. But in 1922 it demanded separation. Northern Ireland chose to remain within the UK. Today, some of the citizens of Northern Ireland call themselves Irish, while others feel more British.

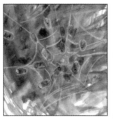 **More than 800 spiders can be found in a square metre of our grassland.** Spiders belong to an ancient group of animals called arachnids and they're an important cog in the world's ecosystem. They help control the number of insects that can destroy plants. As a result, spiders also reduce the need for artificial pesticides. If spiders were wiped out, insect populations would explode, food crops would be decimated, ecological balances would be destroyed and we would all be in a very bad place.

On a less apocalyptic note, spiders spin webs from sticky silk produced by glands in their abdomens. And thanks to the tiny hairs attached to its feet, a spider never gets stuck in its web. After a while, especially if there is no moisture in the air, the web loses its stickiness and the spider often eats it and makes another one. In the past, before plasters were invented, we humans made use of the webs by applying them to our cuts. We knew that the silk of the web, which contains vitamin K, would help clot the blood to reduce bleeding. Today's medical researchers are also interested in the silk, as a material for repairing damaged nerves and tissue in humans.

> "What is this life, if full of care,
> we have no time to stand and stare"
>
> William Henry Davies, poet and tramp

Although they look similar, spiders and insects are very different. Spiders have four rather than three pairs of legs, and two, instead of three, major body sections. Britain has about 660 spider species, of which 280 are the tiny money spiders. Not all spiders spin webs.

Only 17 out of the 37 spider families in Britain build webs in order to catch their prey. These webs have different architectural structures. While a winter morning may reveal a beautiful frosted orb-web, other types include funnel, tangled, lacy, radial, hammock and purse webs.

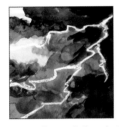

Lightning is hotter than the sun and travels at 220,000,000 miles per hour. Although this is just one third the speed of light, it is still incredibly fast, especially if we think that when we're in a car we might be travelling at a speed of 60mph. Lightning is formed up in the clouds, when ice crystals and droplets of rain bounce around and bump into each other. The friction creates an electrical charge, which builds up until it suddenly discharges. This discharge of electrical energy shows up as lightning – a bit like the white flash and crackly sounds that occur when we pull a synthetic top over our heads.

Most of the lightning is contained inside the clouds, but every now and then some of it shoots out and down to the ground. The bright line we see is only as wide as our finger. As a lightning flash zooms through the air, it makes this air get very hot, very fast, causing it to expand until it explodes. This explosion is the thunder we hear. Sometimes, we don't hear it. This is because light travels faster than sound. So while we can see lightning from many miles away, the sound of the thunder may not reach so far. If we don't hear it, we know that the lightning is a great distance away.

Watching and listening to a thunderstorm is exciting, but lightning can be dangerous. This powerful electrical charge can connect with anything on the ground that conducts electricity, including humans. It is most likely to hit tall objects, such as buildings and trees, which is why we should never seek shelter under a tree and why buildings have a lightning conductor. But if we happen to be outdoors in a storm, a forest may offer more protection than an open field. This is because the risk of a direct lightning strike to a person is higher in a field, since the person is more likely to be the tallest object.

Snowflakes also start life in the clouds. If the temperature inside a cloud is -35°C or lower, tiny droplets of water become frozen and turn into ice crystals. The extreme cold causes them to freeze to other ice crystals and a snowflake is born. In slightly warmer clouds, the frozen droplets are unable to stick together and instead form around a particle of dust or pollen. As they fall through the dry, cool air as small, powdery snowflakes, they create dry snow.

All snowflakes have six sides, but every one is unique. This is because there is an infinite number of possible shapes they can form as they fall. But it is a myth that the temperature needs to be below 0°C to snow. In fact, the heaviest snowfalls in the UK occur when the air temperature is between 0°C and 2°C. When it is a little above 0°C we get wet snow. The snowflakes melt around the edges and stick to other snowflakes. They become big, heavy flakes – perfect for making

"I wonder if the snow loves the trees and fields, that it kisses them so gently? And then it covers them up snug, you know, with a white quilt"

Lewis Carroll, author of *Alice in Wonderland*

snowballs. If the temperature is above 2°C, the snowflakes melt and fall as sleet rather than snow. If it is warmer still, we get rain. In the UK, Scotland's Cairngorms mountain range gets the most snow or sleet, while Cornwall in England has the least.

Many plants, insects and animals have been imported into England and the UK from other countries. Sometimes, these non-native species have a negative impact on our native species. In the 1870s the grey squirrel was brought over from North America as a fashionable decoration for large estates. People never imagined that over time it would drive our red squirrel population to near-extinction, since the greys are bigger, stronger and more resilient to disease. Measures have since been taken to create a healthier balance between the two species, but many grey squirrels continue to be slaughtered. Better to be careful what we wish for.

It's a similar story with the seven-spot ladybird. Most of us are familiar with this much-loved insect, but we may not know that there are around 45 ladybird species in Britain. Not all are red and some have up to 24 spots. In 2004, however, the harlequin ladybird arrived. A native of China, Japan and Russia, it was introduced into the United States in 1988 as an environmentally friendly means of pest control. Confusingly, it, too, can have anything from two spots to 21. Having spread to Europe and our shores, the harlequin now competes with the smaller seven-spot for food and will sometimes eat it.

Some may argue that the squirrels and ladybirds are simply playing out Darwin's natural selection theory. Darwin was an English biologist who lived in the 19th century. He was the first to come up with this idea of "the survival of the fittest", which basically means that the species most adaptable to change pulls through. But even if nature and evolution are indeed taking their course in the case of the squirrels and ladybirds, people are still guilty of having interfered in the first place.

> "Man selects only for his own good;
> nature only for that of the being which she tends"
>
> Charles Darwin, naturalist and biologist

Although they are up against humans, perhaps it is not too late to save Britain's hedgehogs. Experts say the fall in numbers is caused by fewer foraging and nesting sites. With their town and countryside habitats disappearing, hedgehogs are finding it more difficult to come across food and mates. They need to travel up to a mile a night, too, so continuous habitat is crucial for them. We can help by making small gaps in fencing to allow hedgehogs to pass, avoiding the use of pesticides and slug pellets in our gardens, and putting out dishes of water during dry spells. Hedgehog charities also recommend creating homes with piles of logs and leaving part of our gardens wild.

THANK YOU

To all the people who, knowingly and unknowingly, helped to create this book.

My parents My mother passed on her love of English poetry and literature. She also taught me that it's never too late or too soon to dive into something new. When he is not running, my father has the ability to sit still and look and smell and listen. Many little but precious things have reached me this way too.

My grandparents They encouraged me to doodle and splash about with paints. Grandma was strict and did sparkling watercolours. Grandpa did moody oil paintings and traipsed across hills and fields, unearthing fossils, birds' nests and other treasures. Both knew the names of all our wild flowers, trees and birds.

A very special aunt Also the former owner of a very special old rectory and garden, where I was lucky enough to spend my summers. Her generosity and passion for wildlife and gardening threw a rainbow of colour over many people.

My best friend His knowledge of all kinds of subjects inspired me to research and write the *Worth knowing* section of this book. He also gave me the idea for the *Eco Warrior* poem, since he has few possessions and darns his socks.

The rain-or-shine hiking organiser Without countless explorations of England's shires and other glorious parts of the UK, I would be much the poorer in mind, body and spirit.

My book designer Thanks to her artistic and technical skills, problem solving and patience, the result is a sensitive combination of illustrations and wording. I gladly provide her contact details here. Susanna Hickling: susannahickling@gmail.com

I am grateful to the following experts for ensuring this book is factually correct: Prof. Nick Colegrave, chair in experimental evolution, School of Biological Sciences, The University of Edinburgh; Dr Nigel Reeve, ecologist and hedgehog specialist.